I love my doggy coloring book

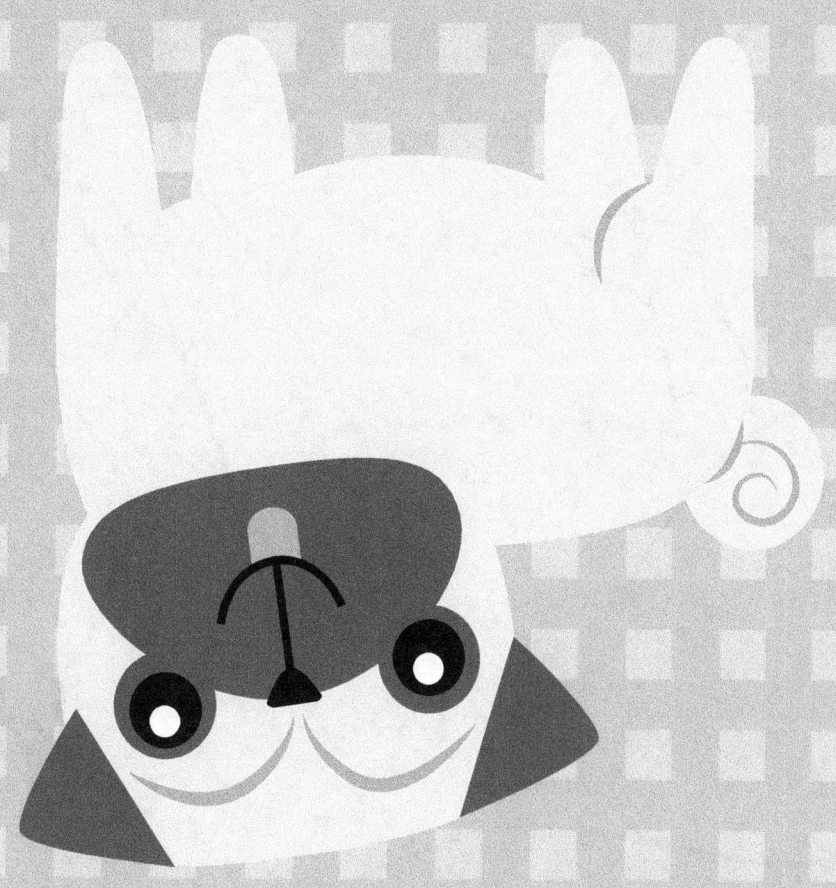

By: Jayden Madrid-Kitchen

DO YOU SPEAK ANIMAL?

Some dogs like to play.

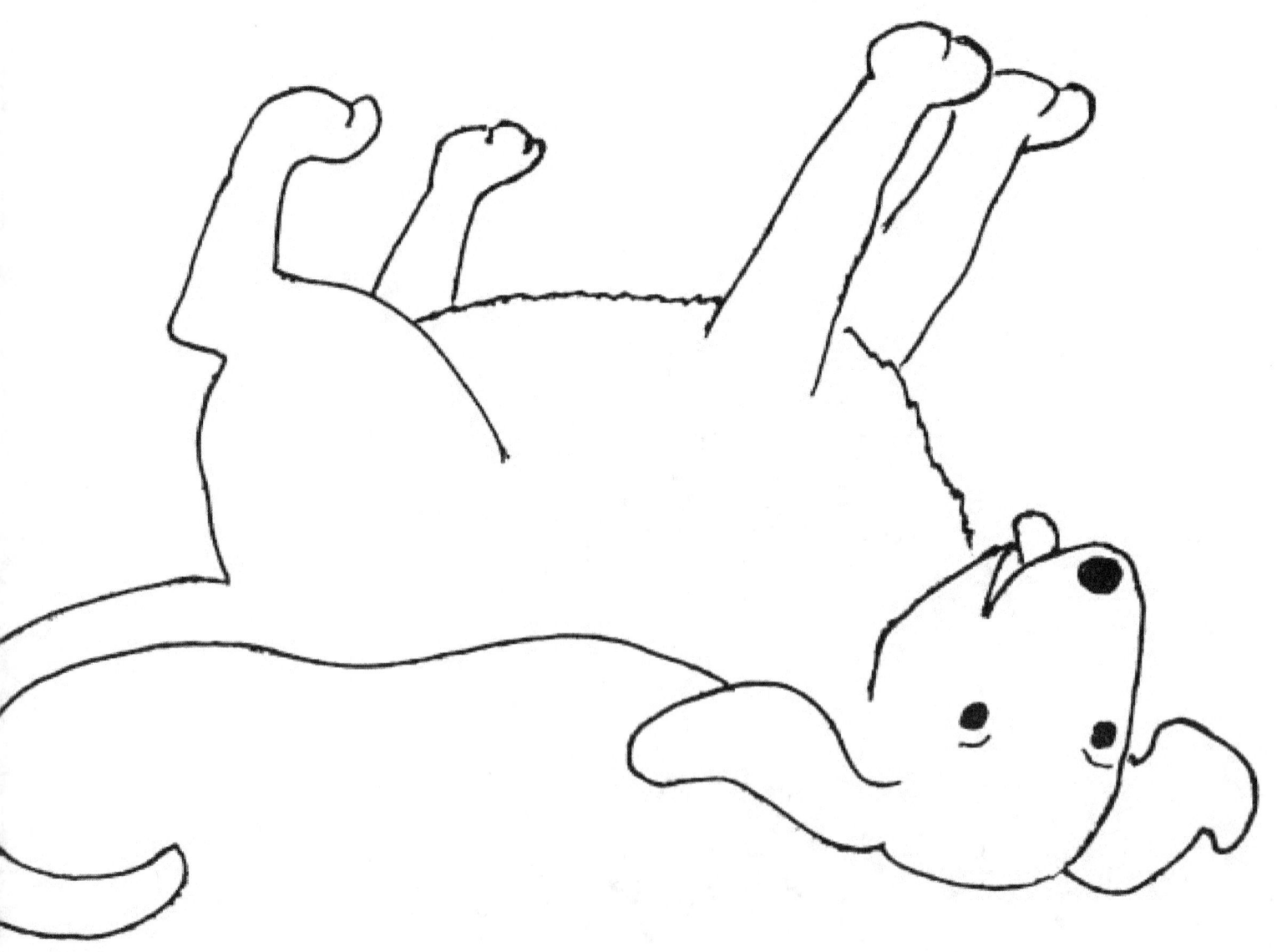

Some dogs are big and lovable.

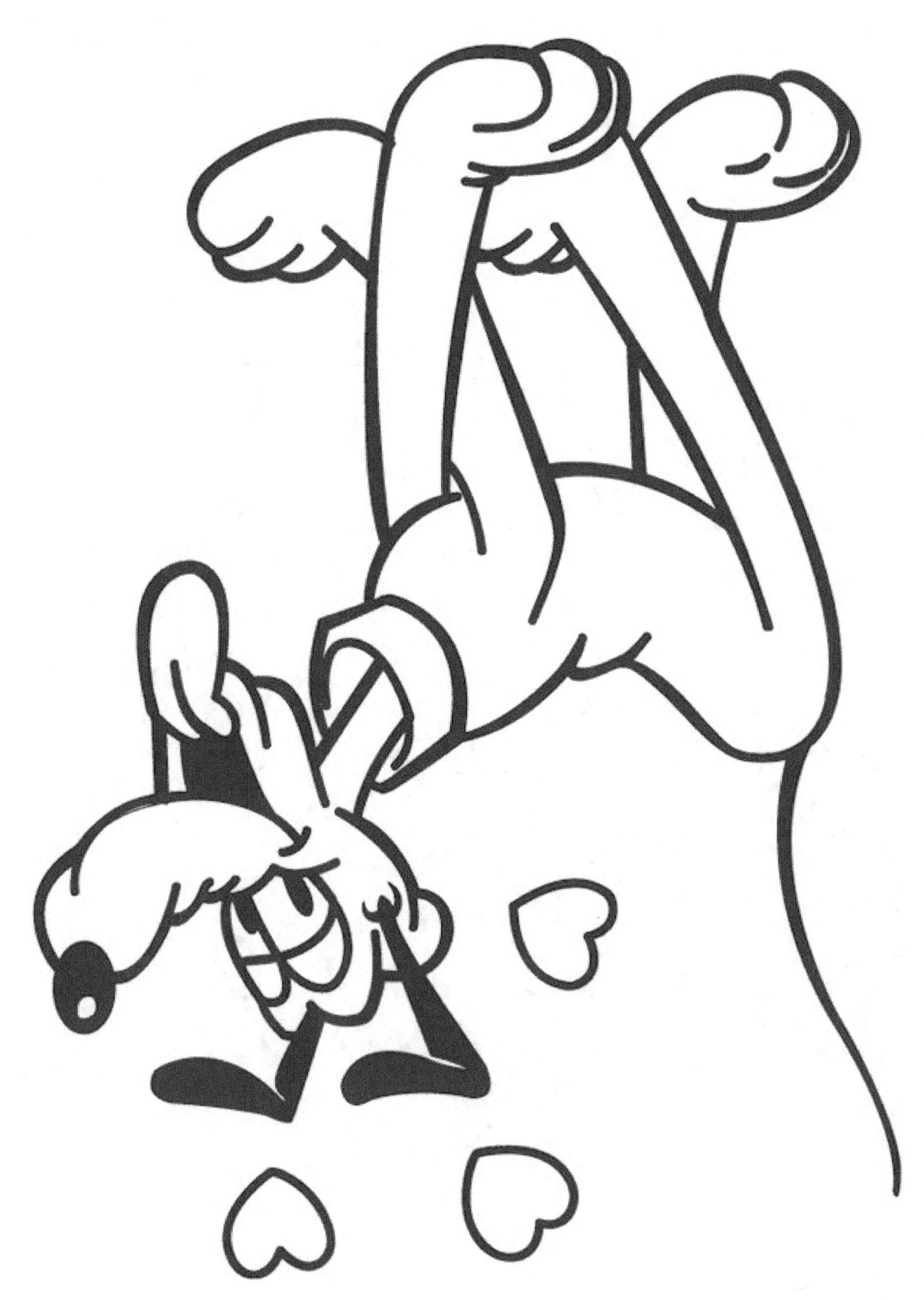

Sometimes doggies have friends.

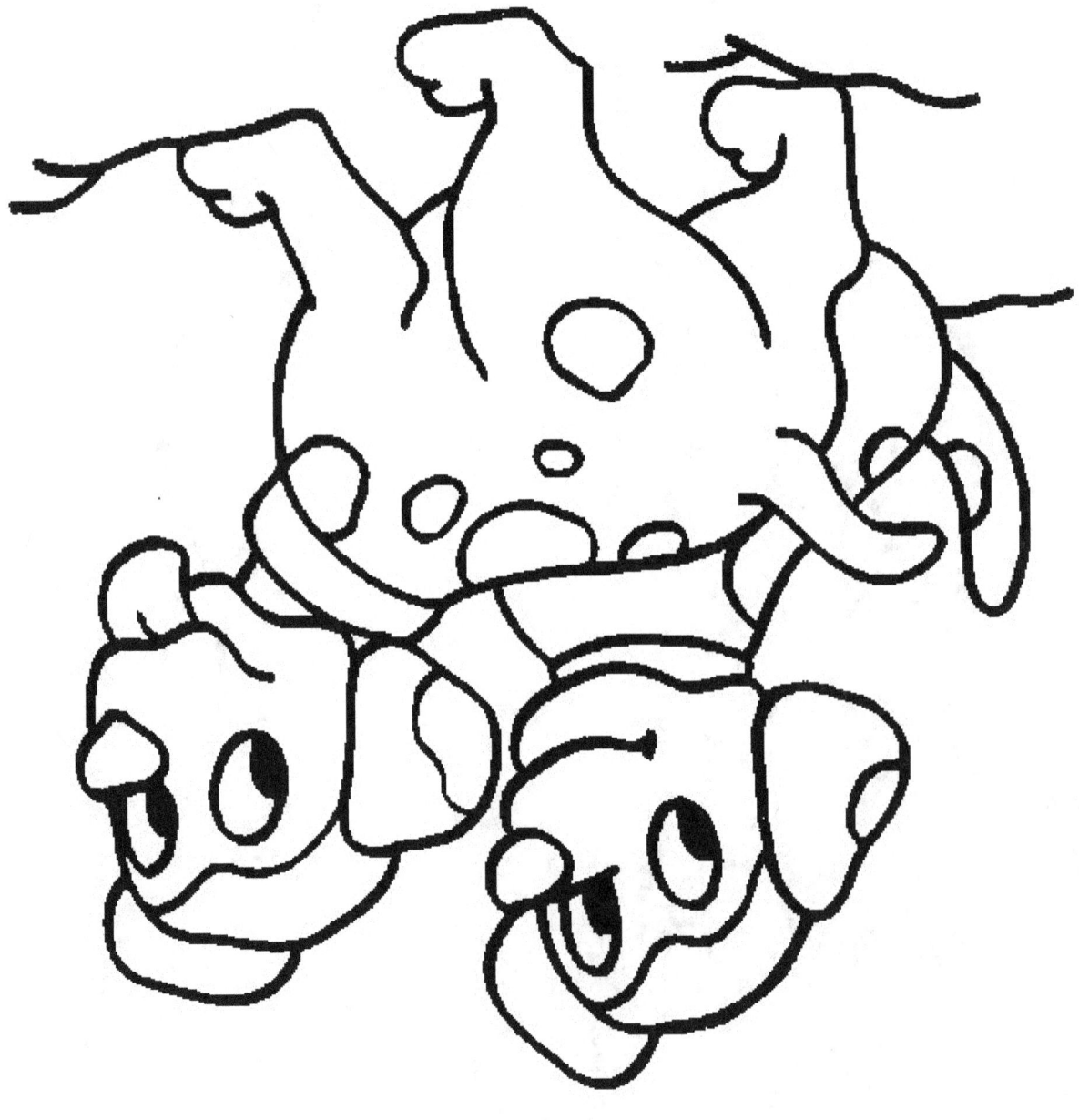

Some doggies wear sombreros

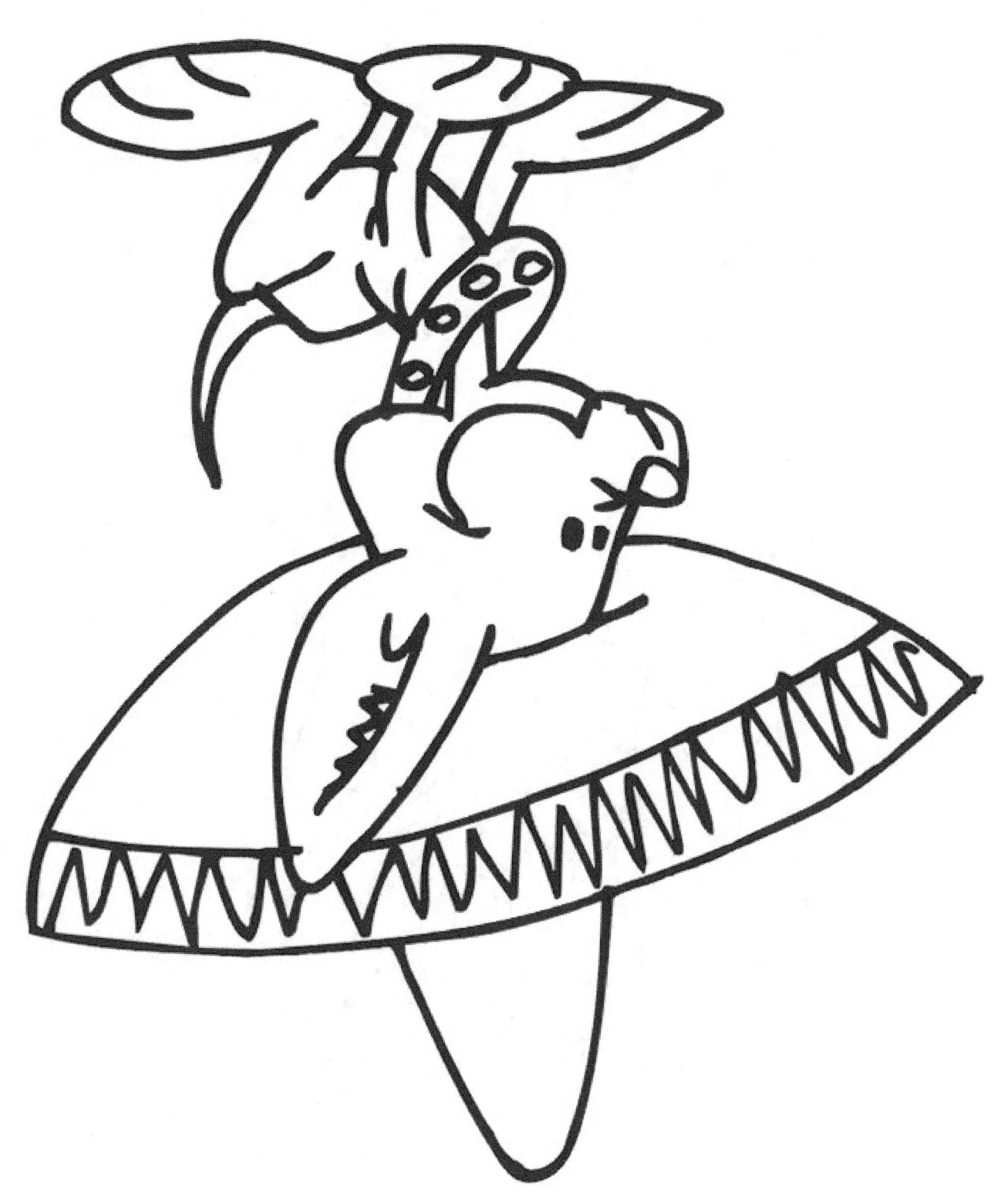

Some dogs need nap time.

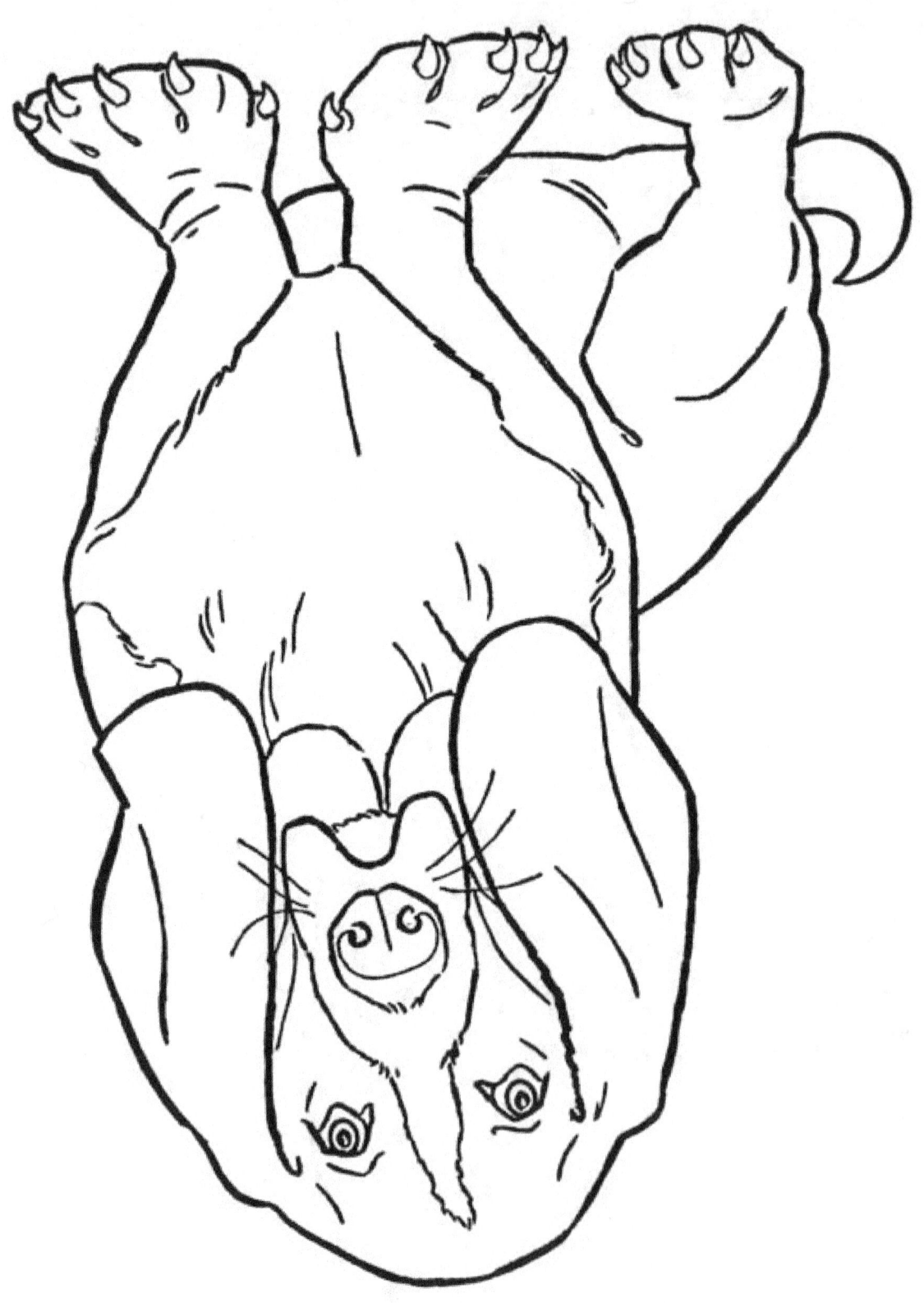

Some doggies like to share.

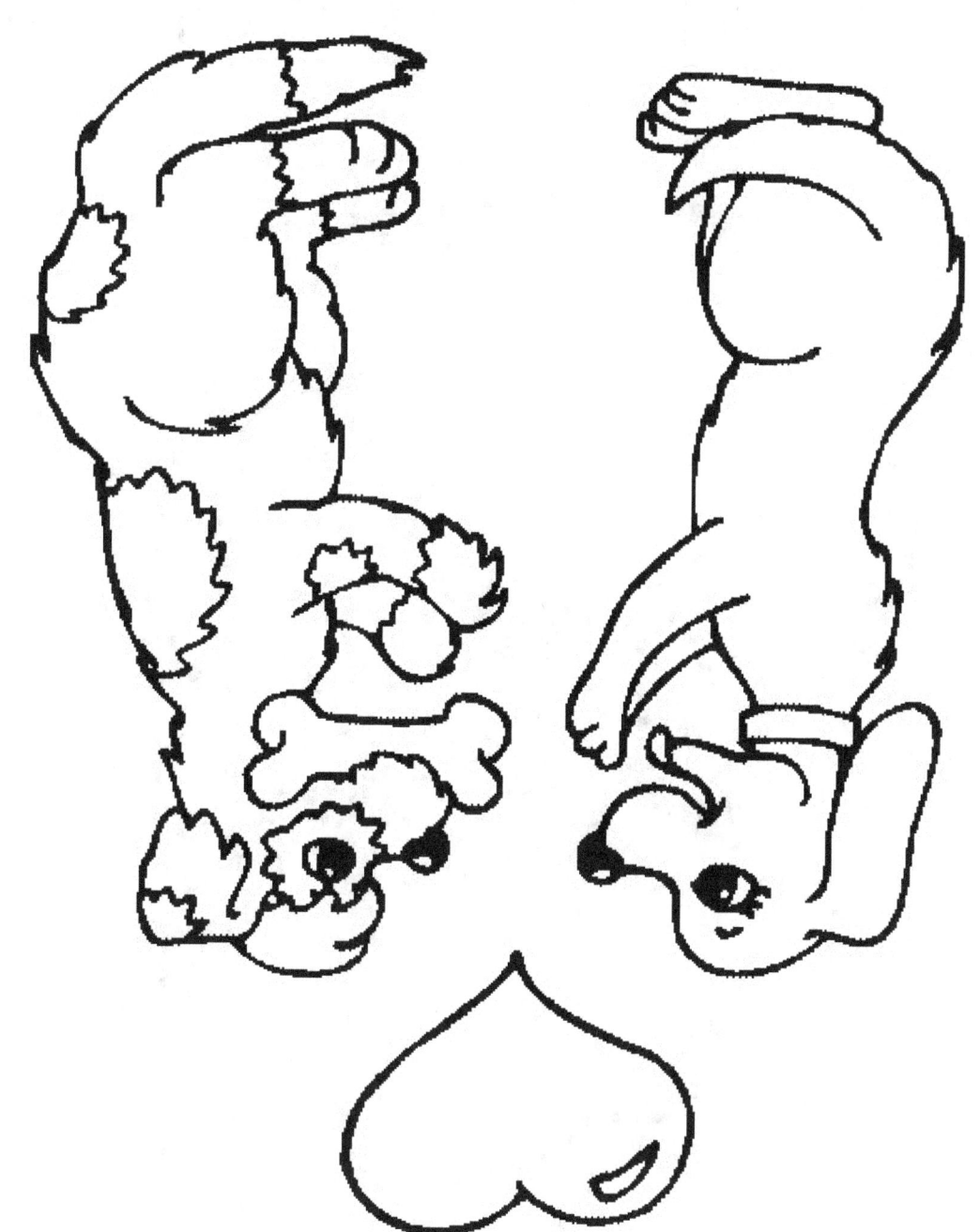

Some doggies don't like to share...

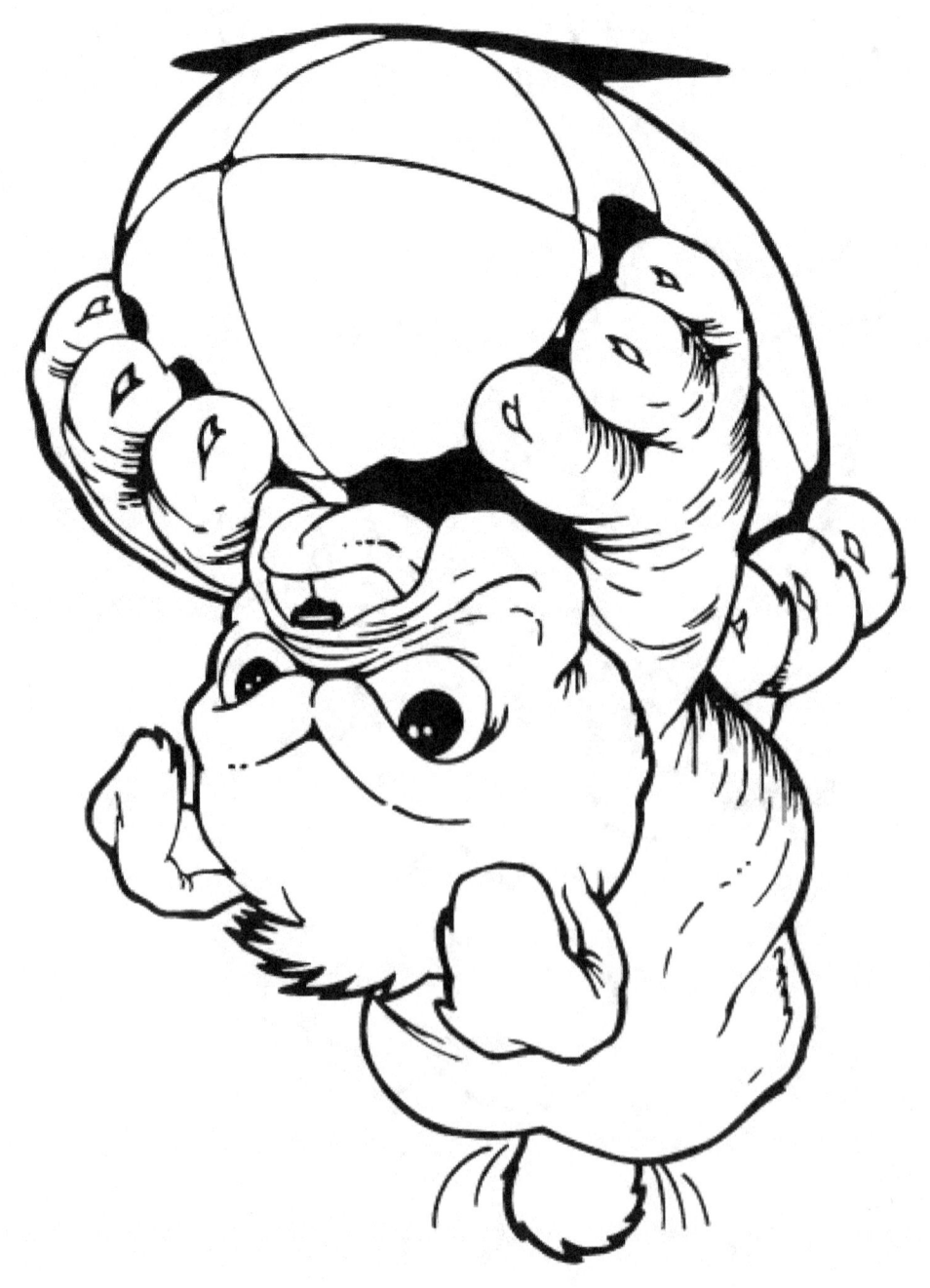

Some doggies like their blanky.

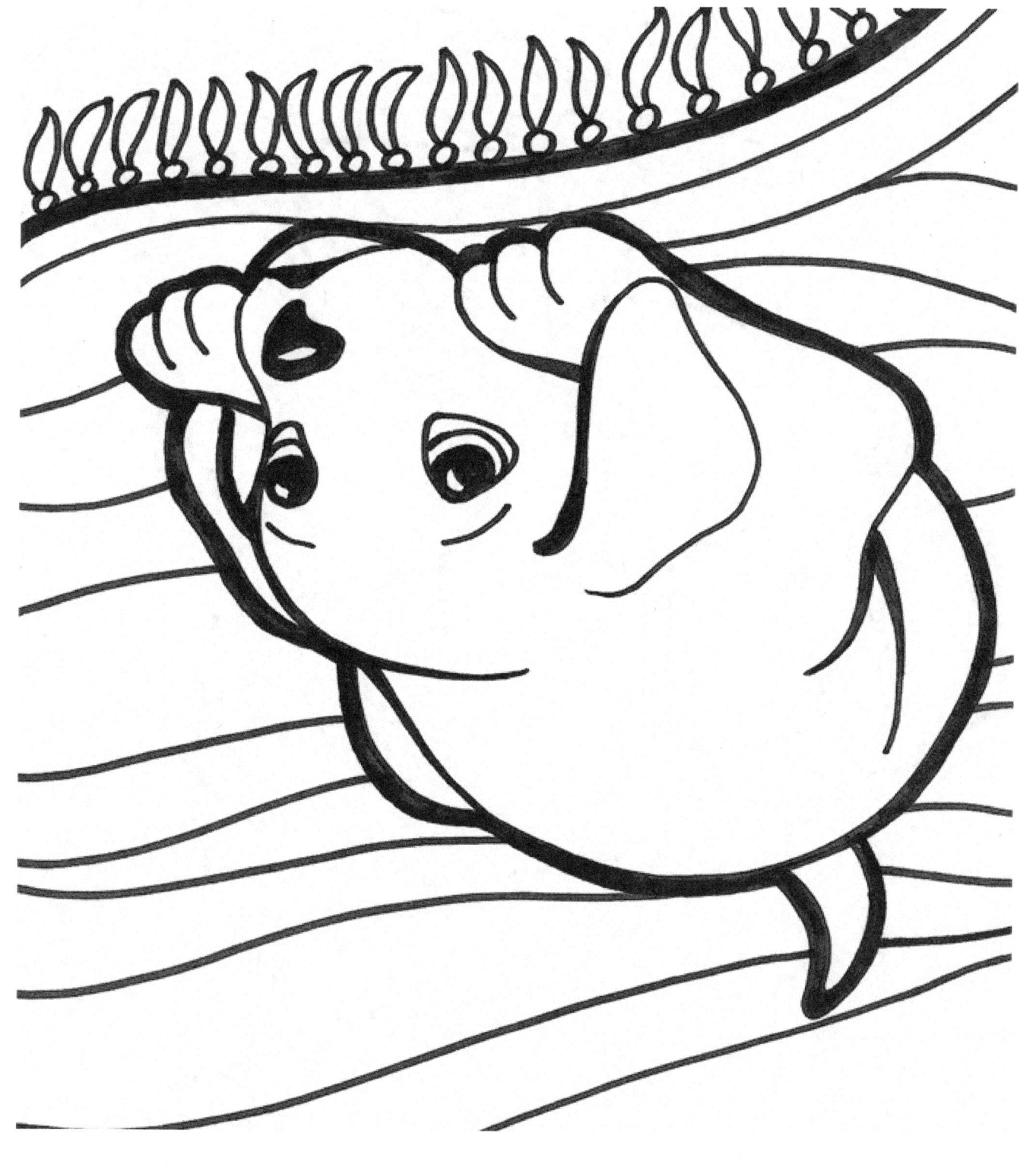

Some doggies like to chew on shoes

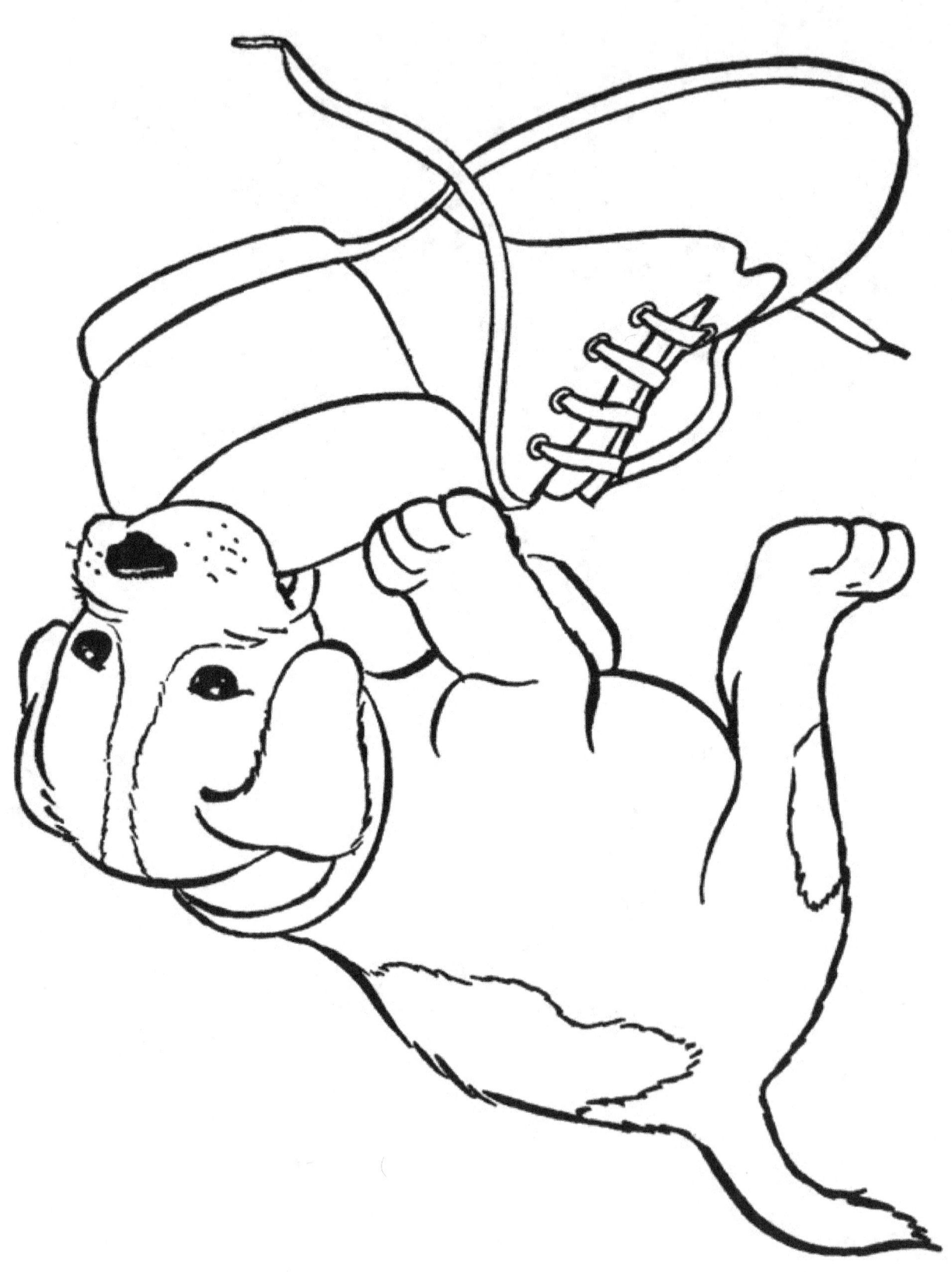

Some doggies like to play.

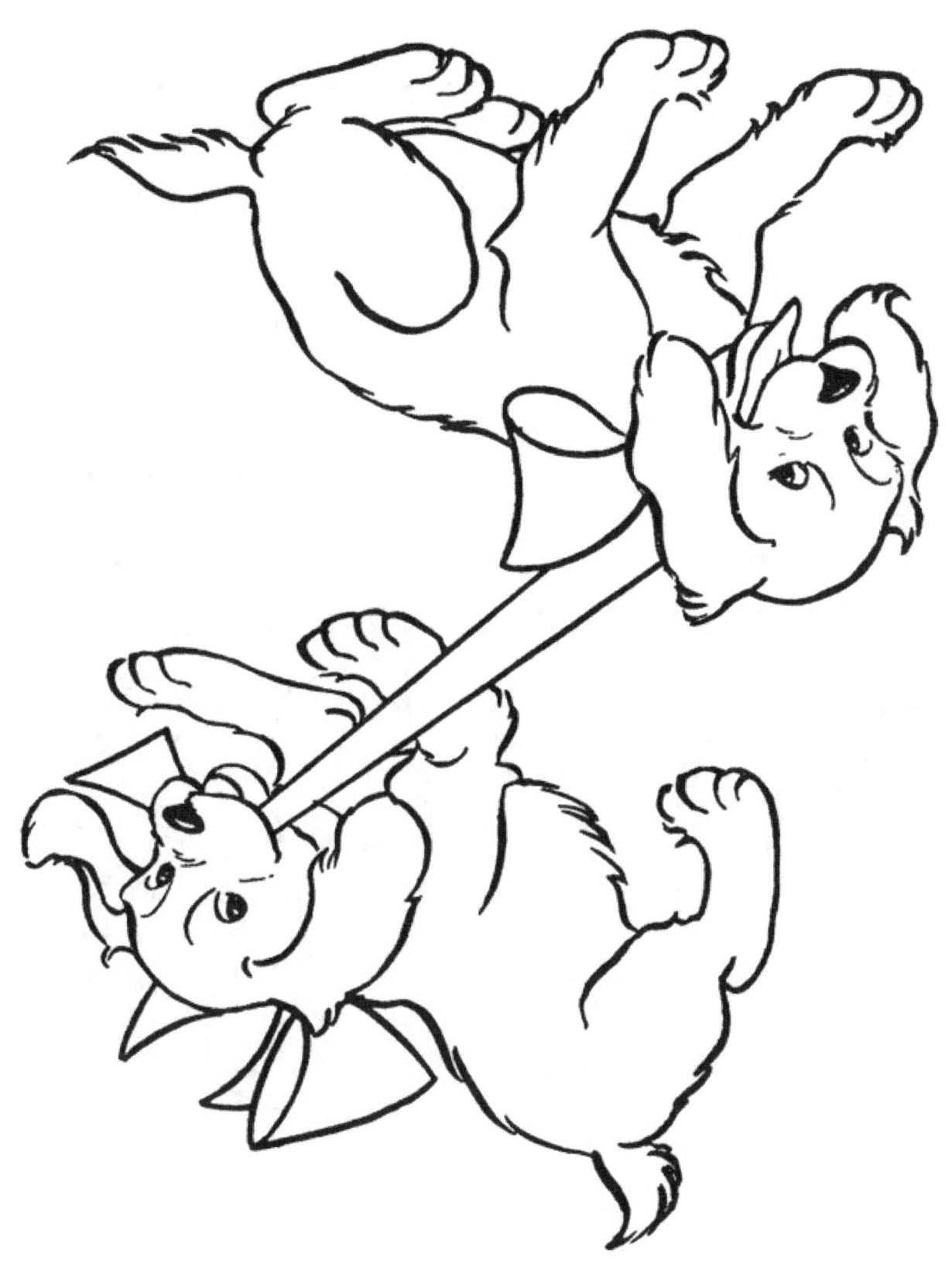

Some doggies love to be outdoors.

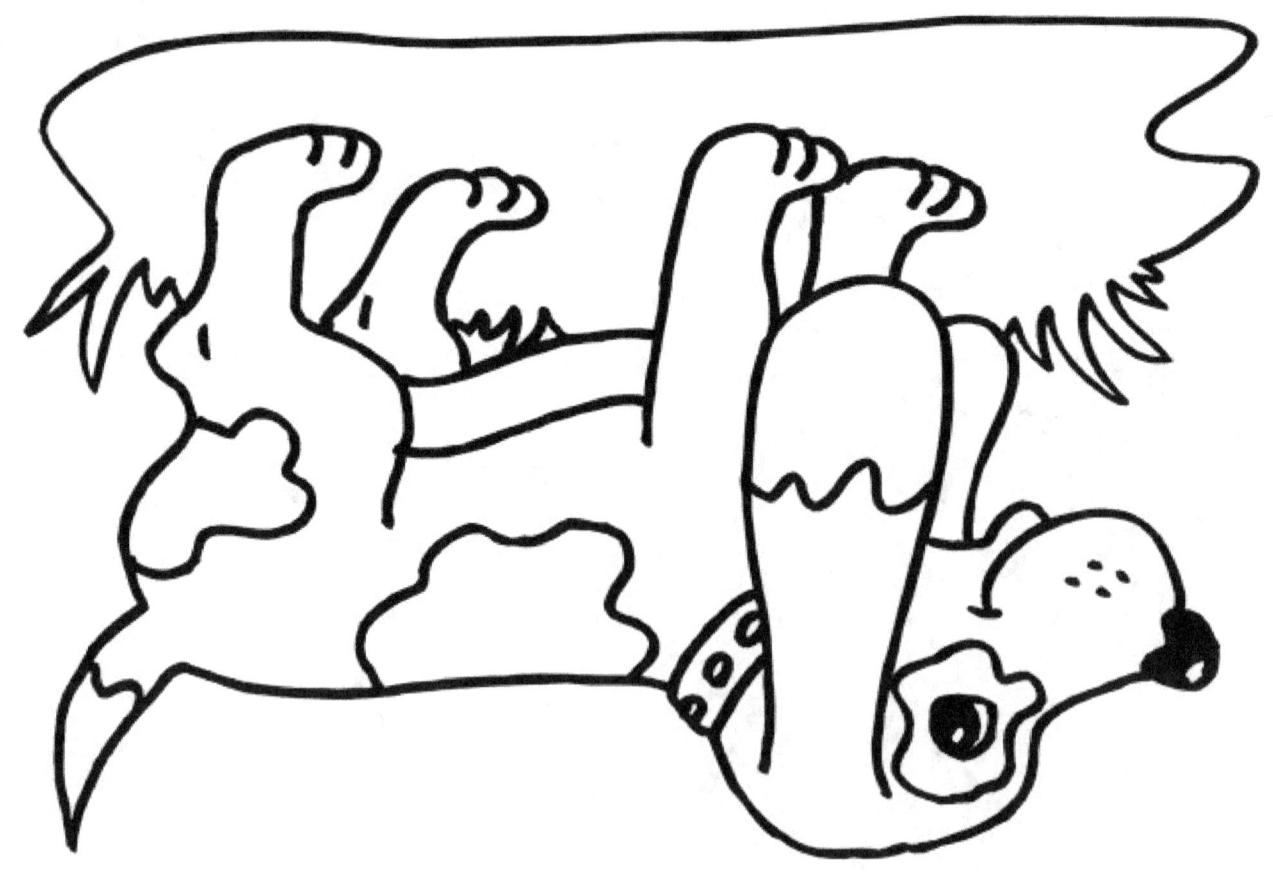

Some doggies are big and fat.

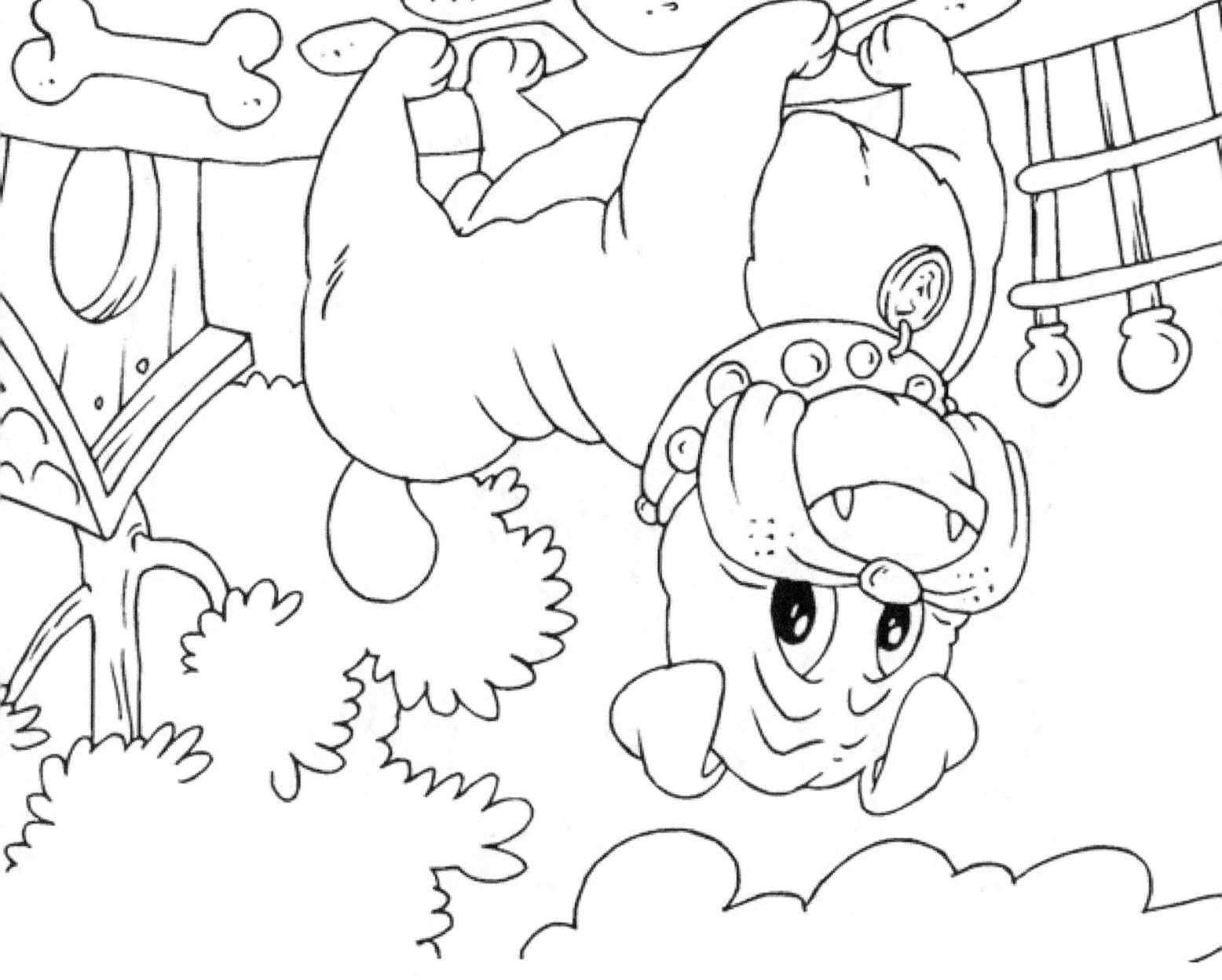

Some doggies get into everything.

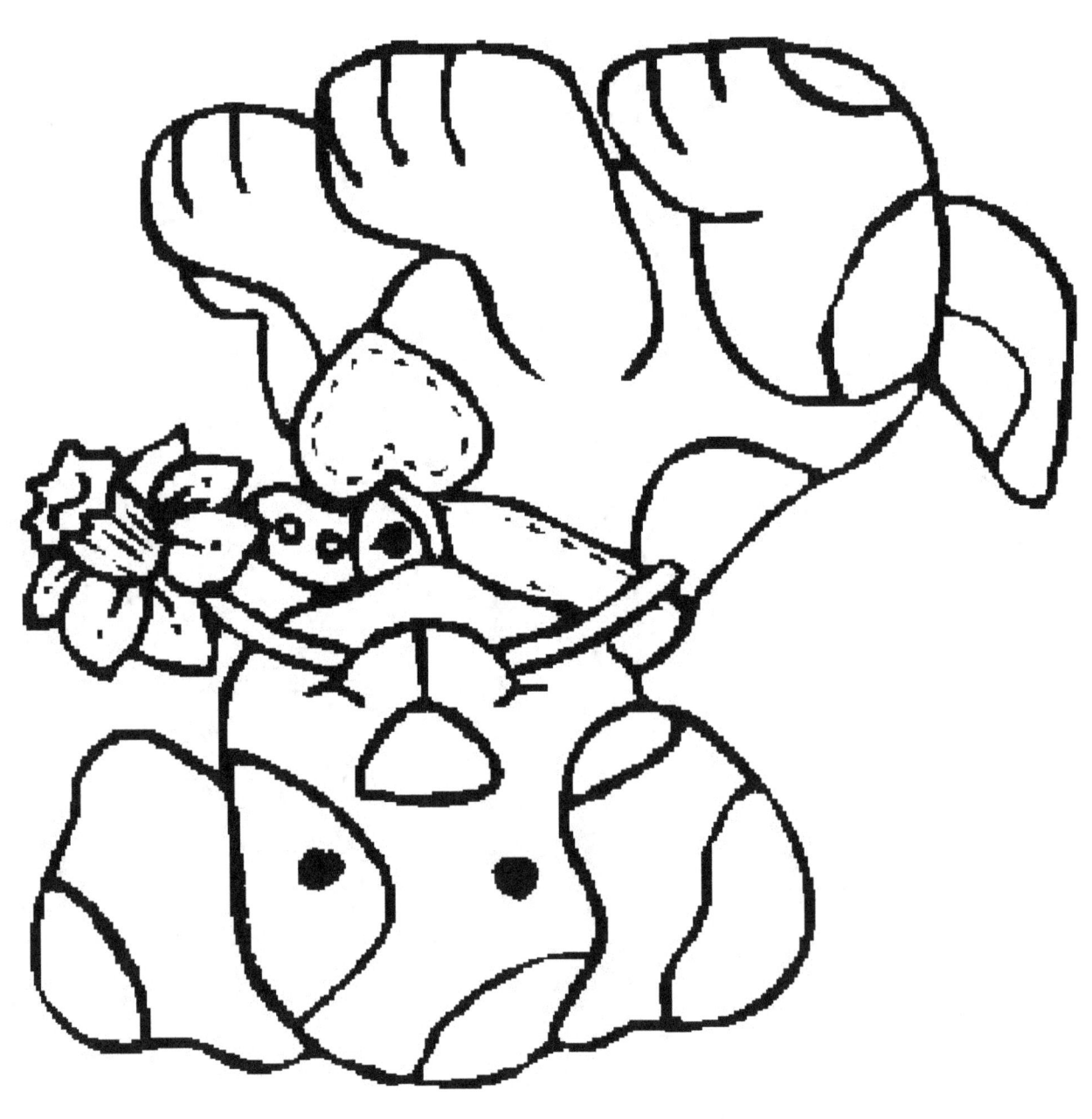

Some doggies love to play chase.

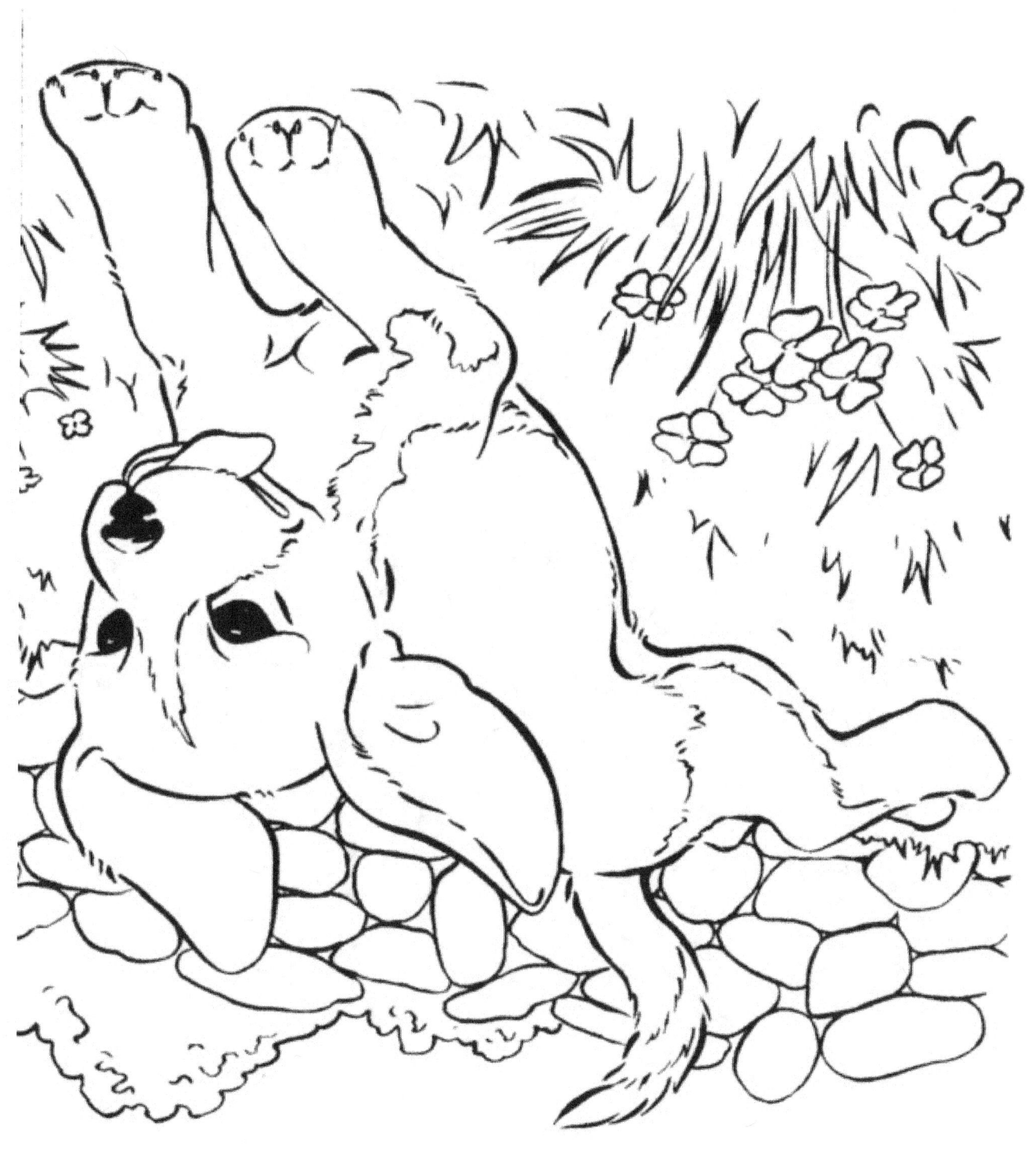

Some doggies love popcorn.

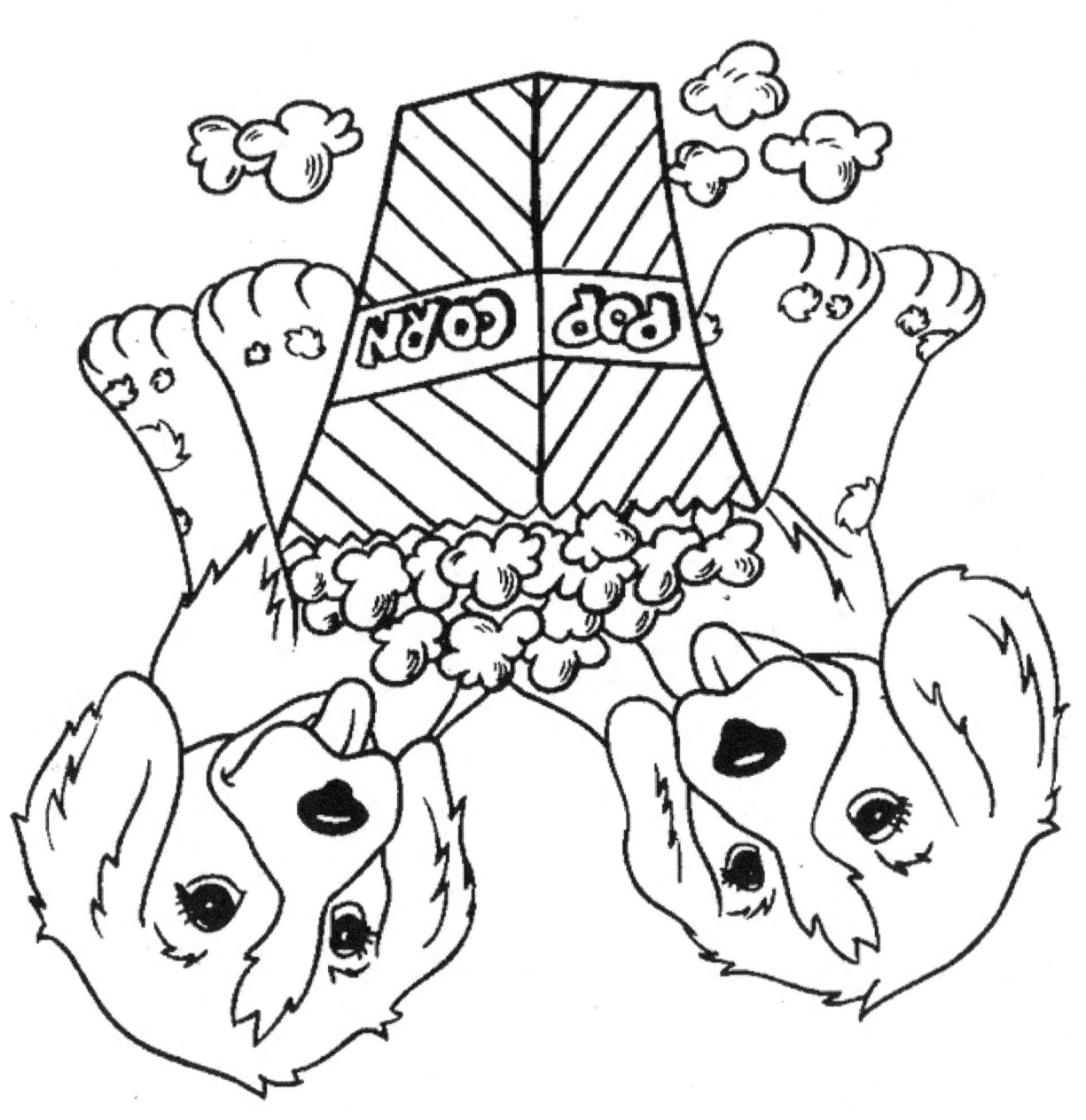

Some doggies have a happy face.

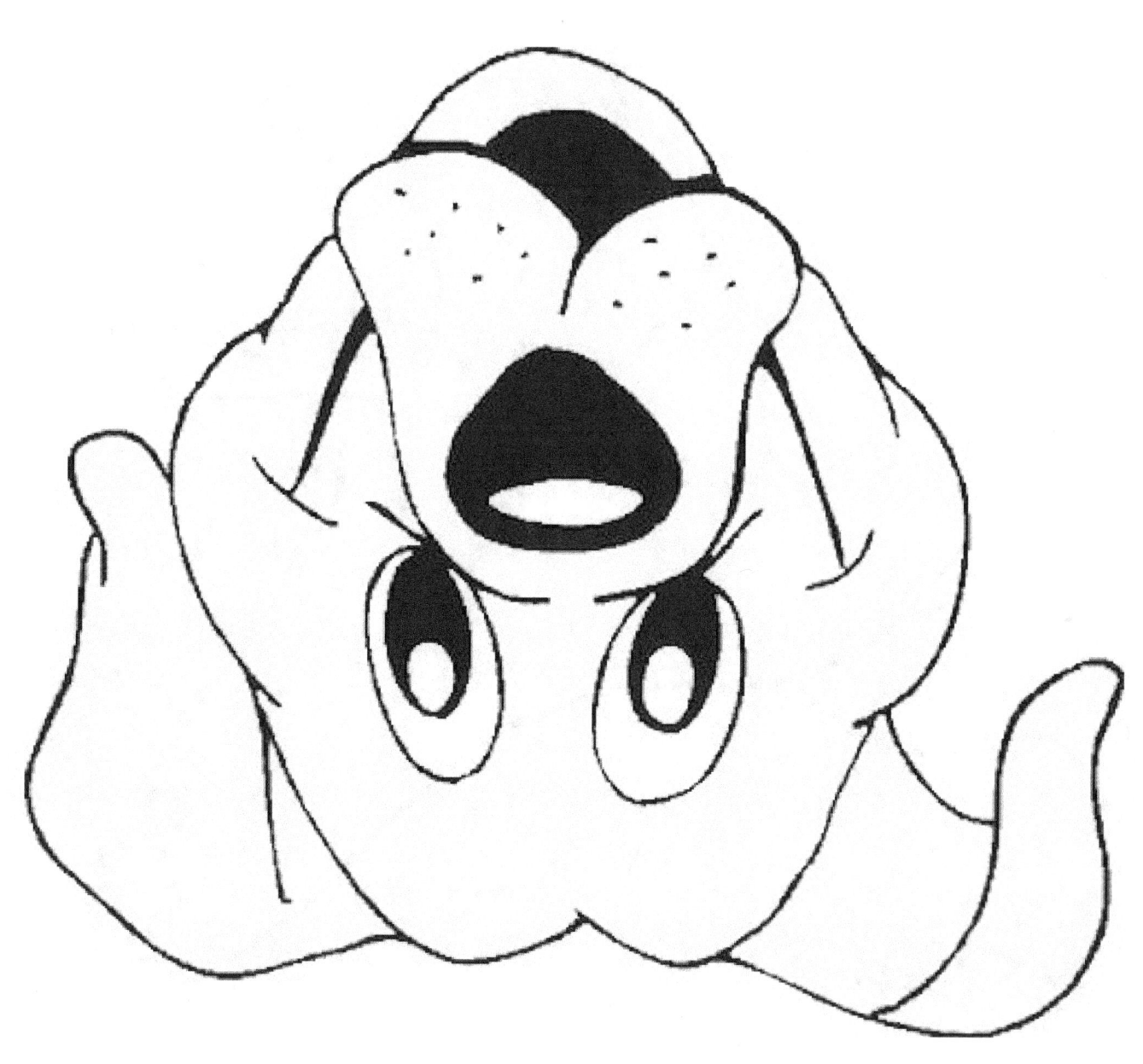

Some doggies are big.

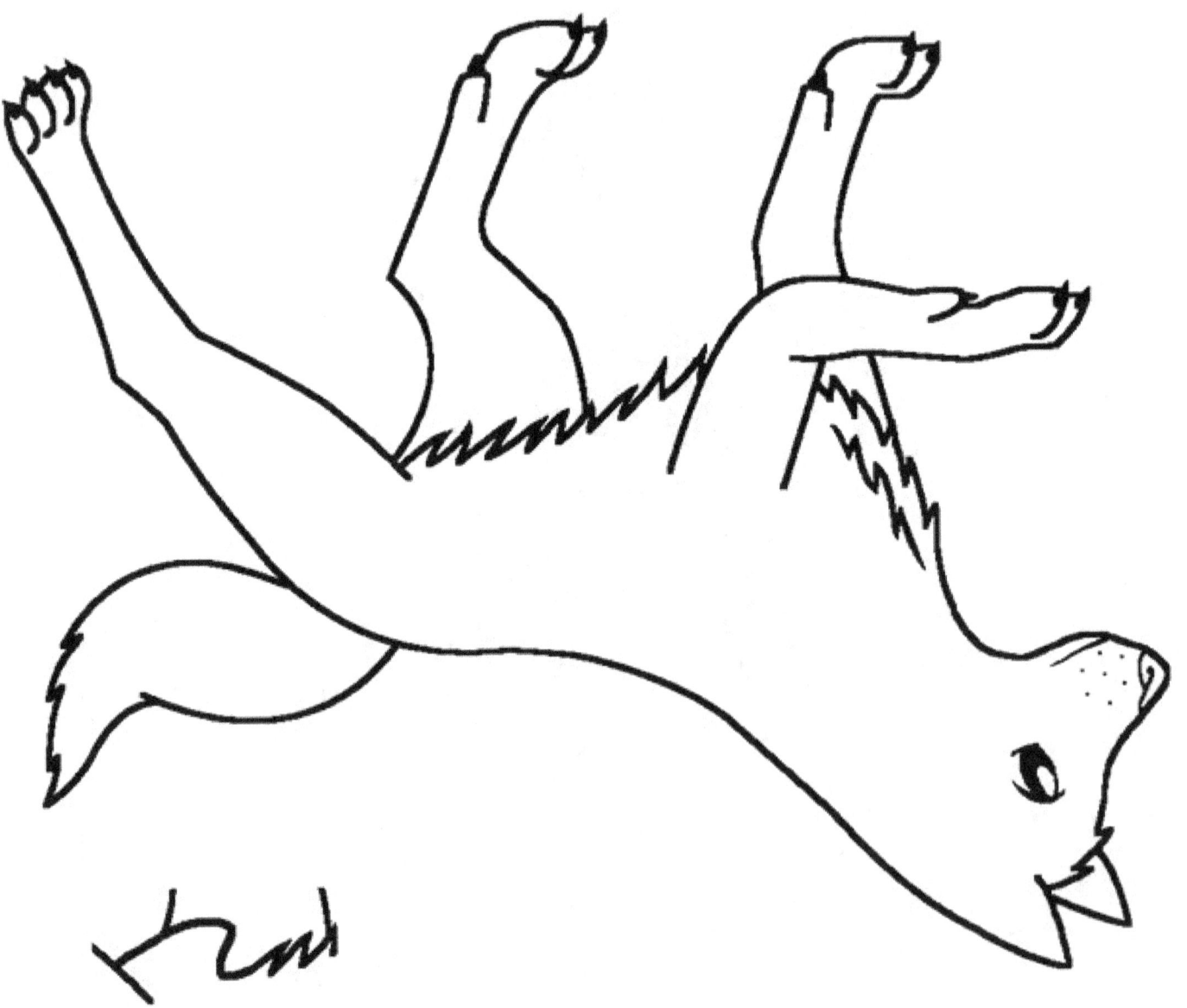

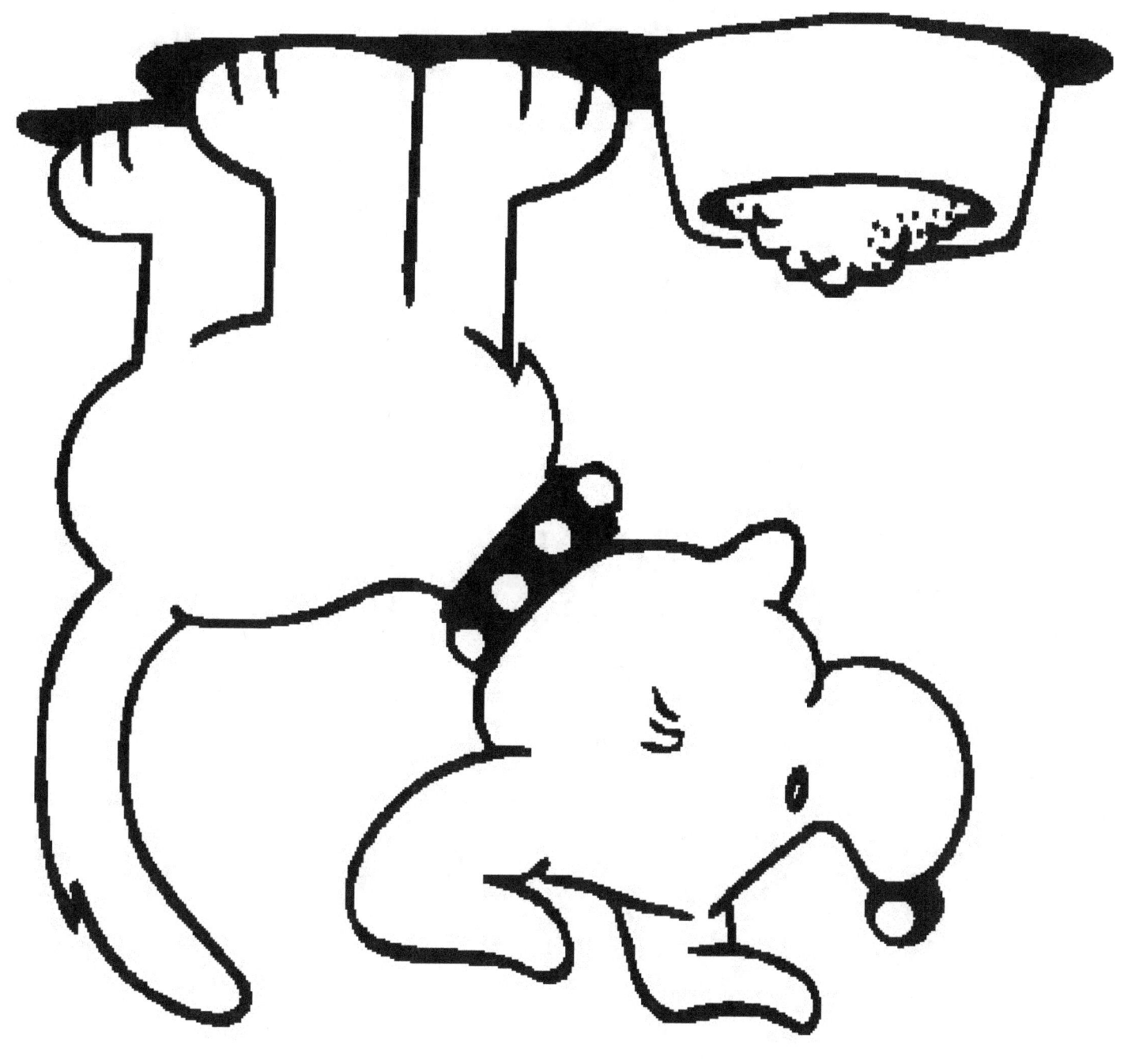

My doggie loves to eat.

Some doggies need mommy.

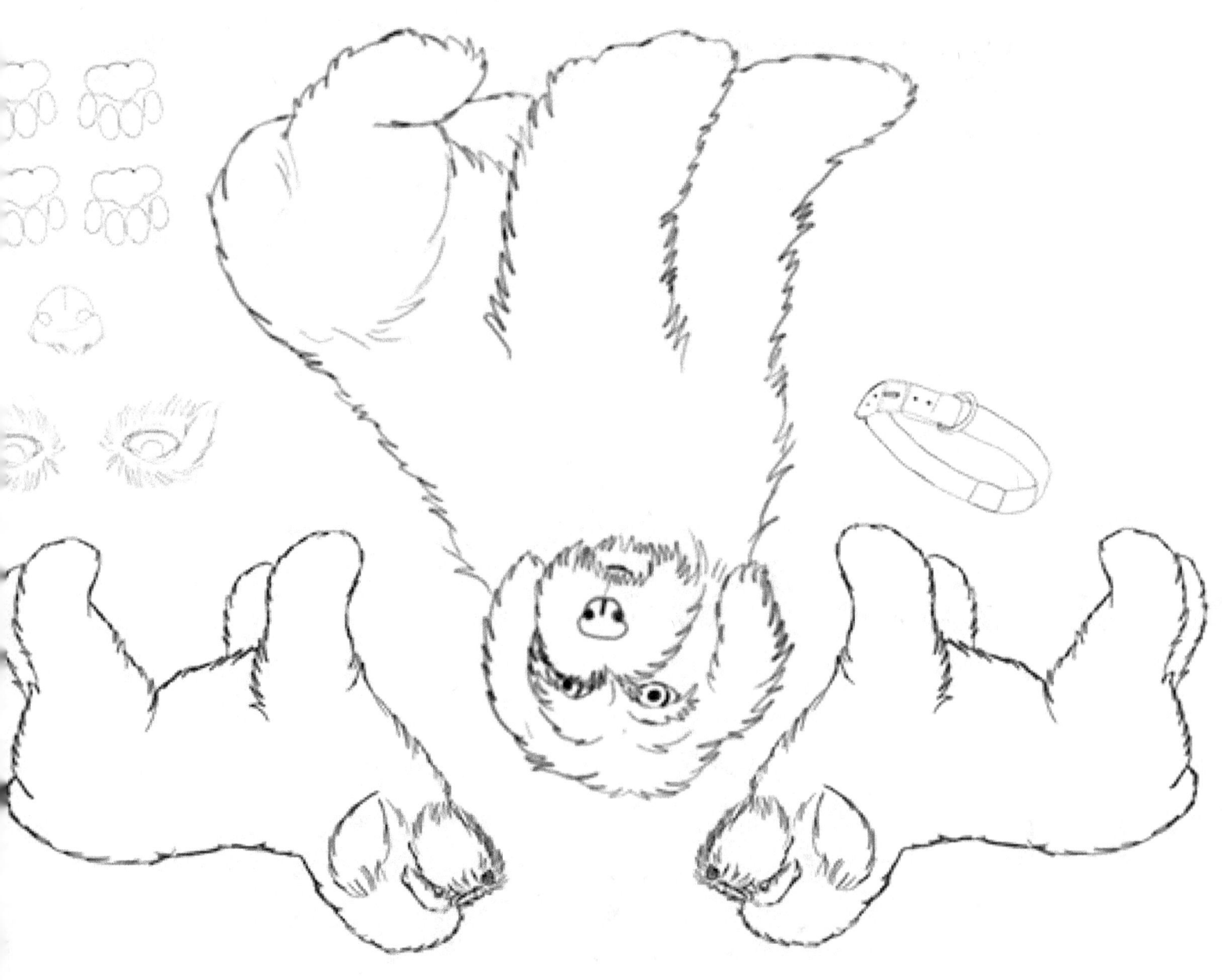

Some doggies look just alike.

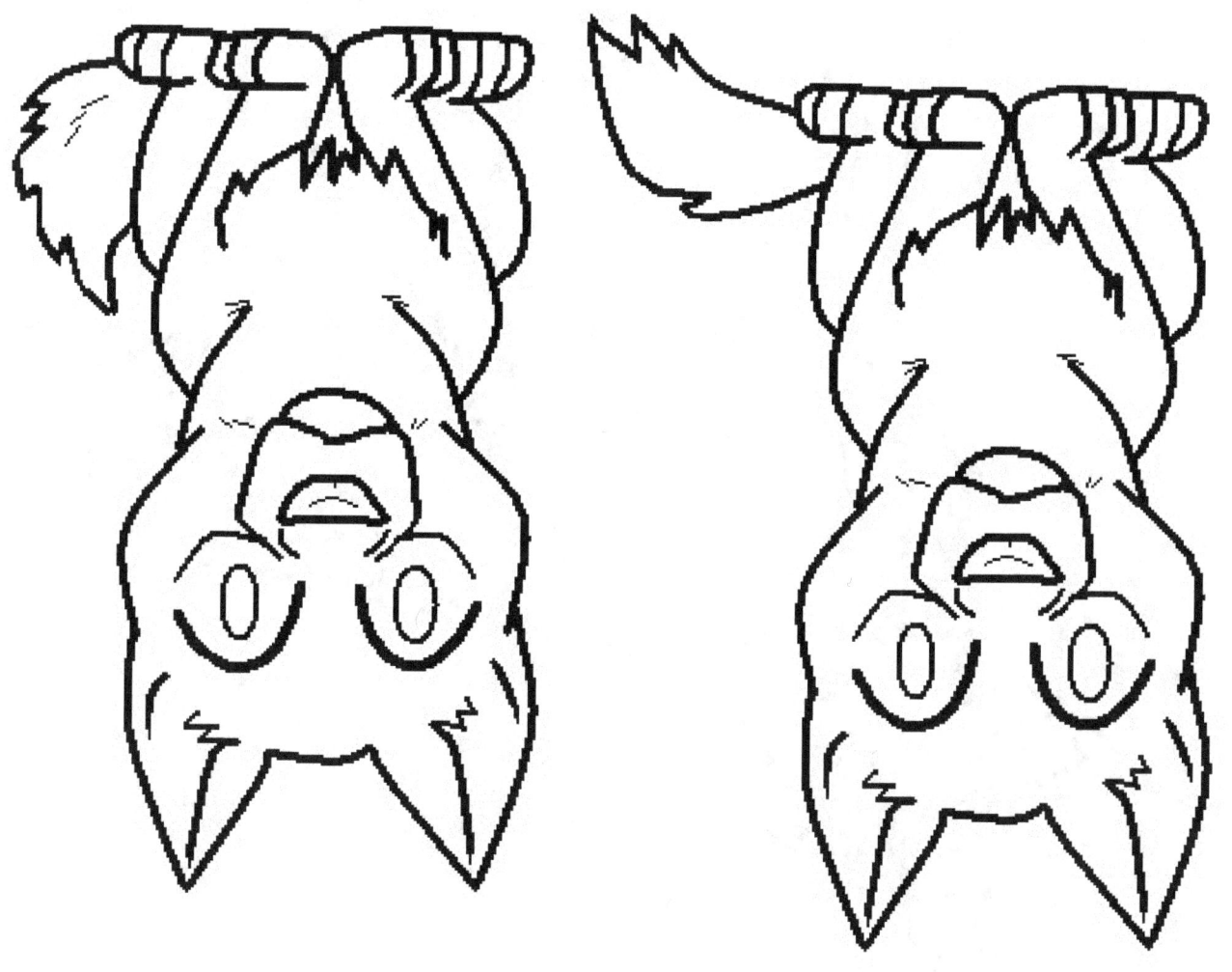

Some doggies look like ponies

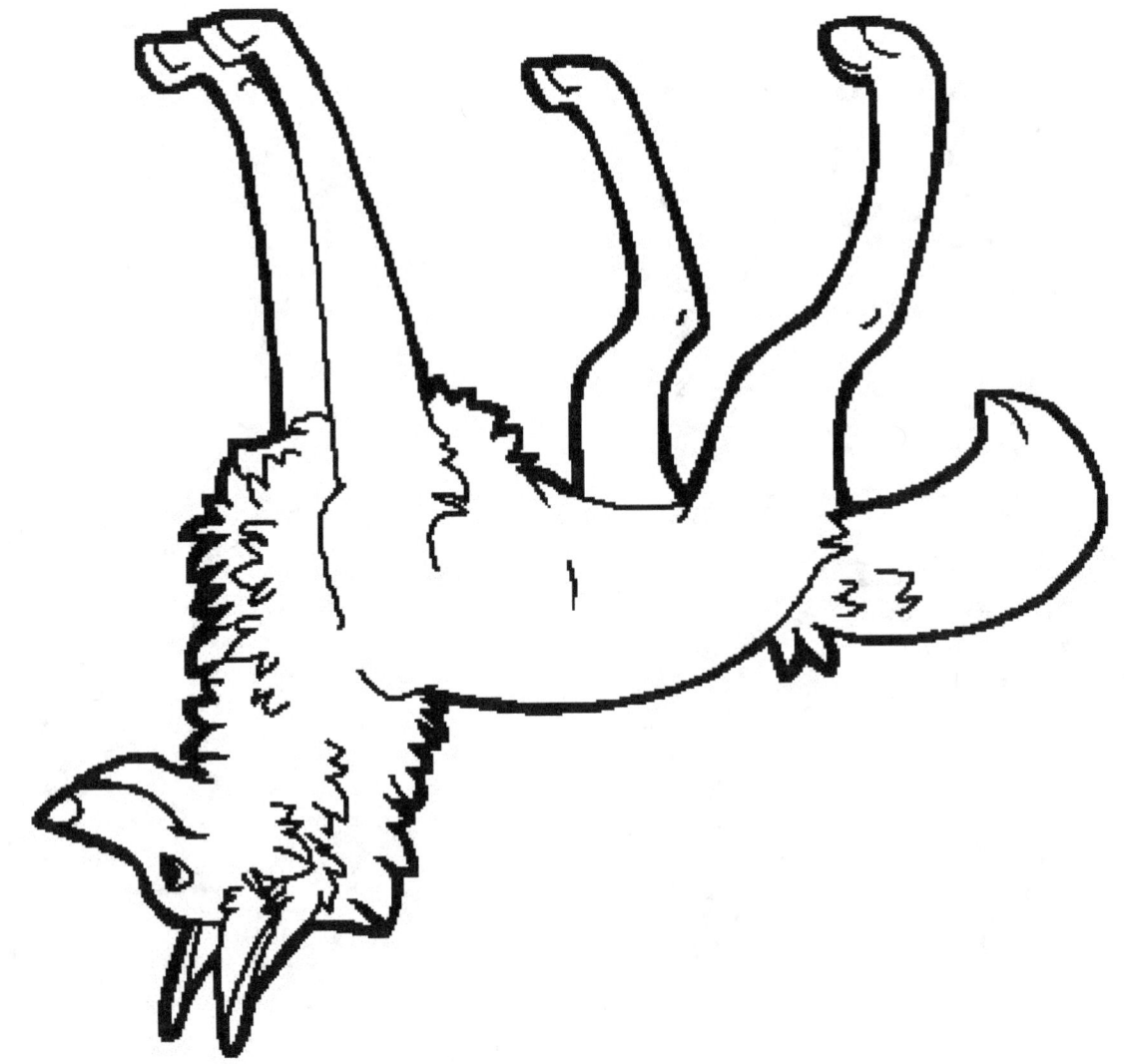

Some doggies are fluffy.

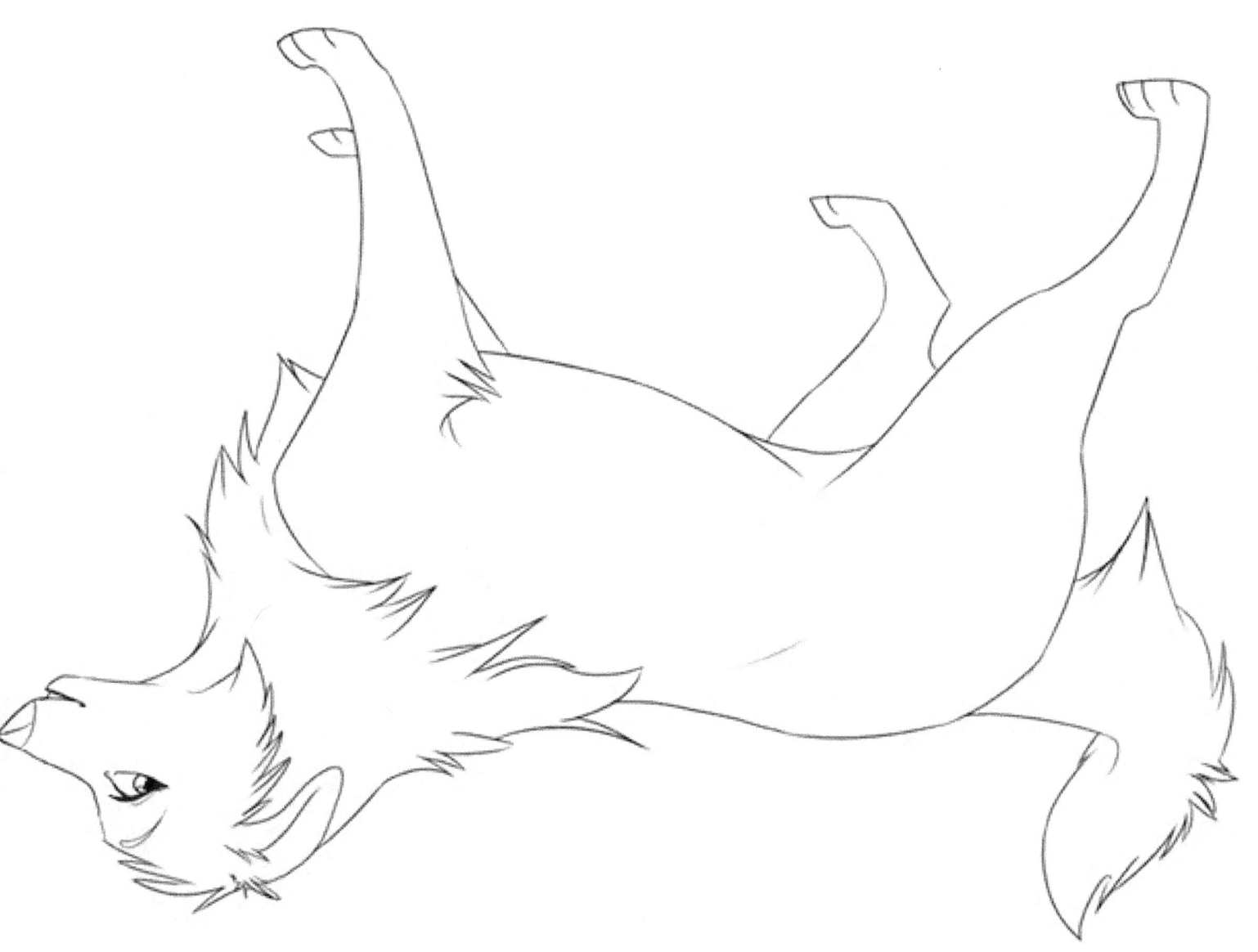

Some doggies have big ears and some doggies have small ears

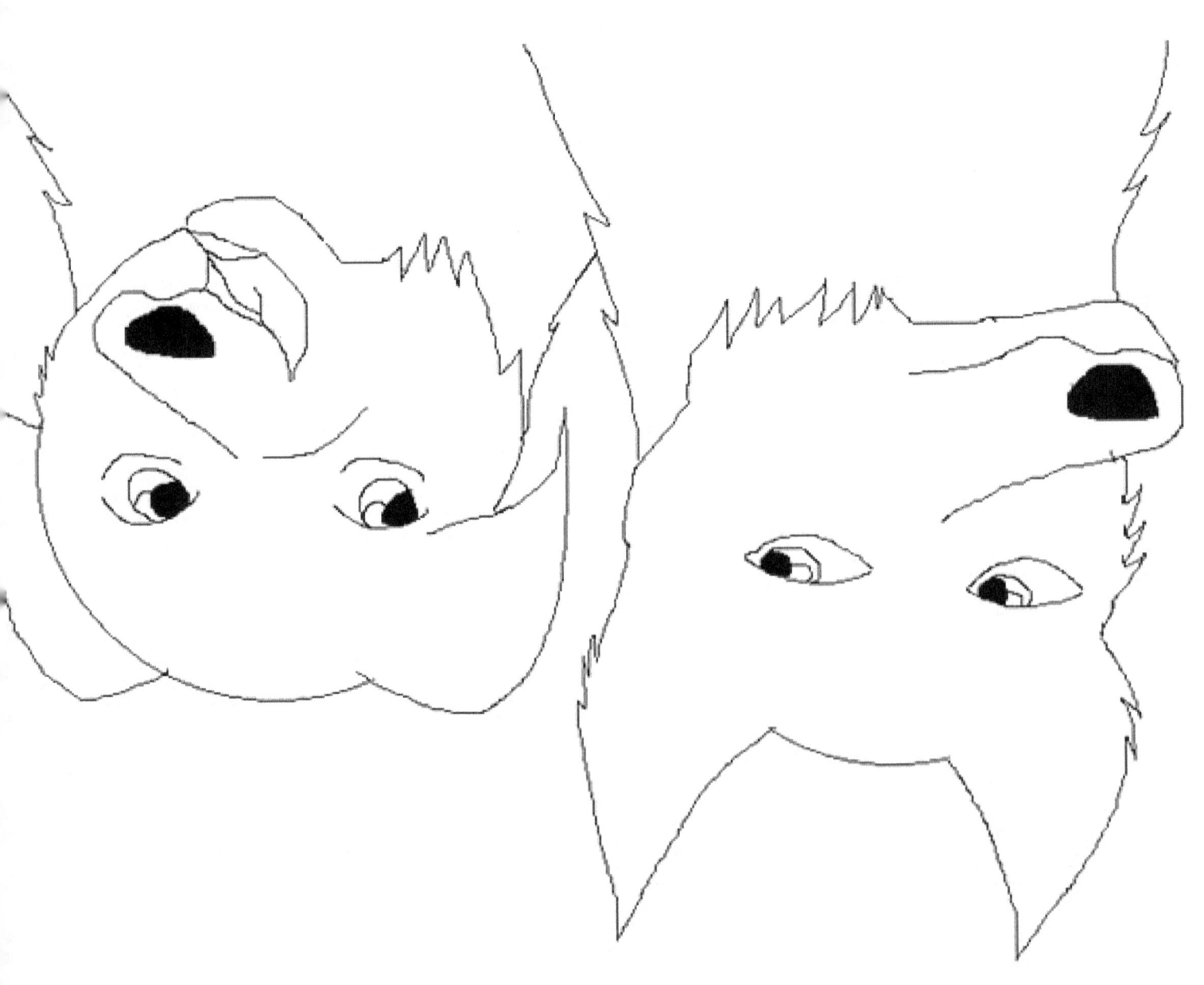

My doggie is my best friend.

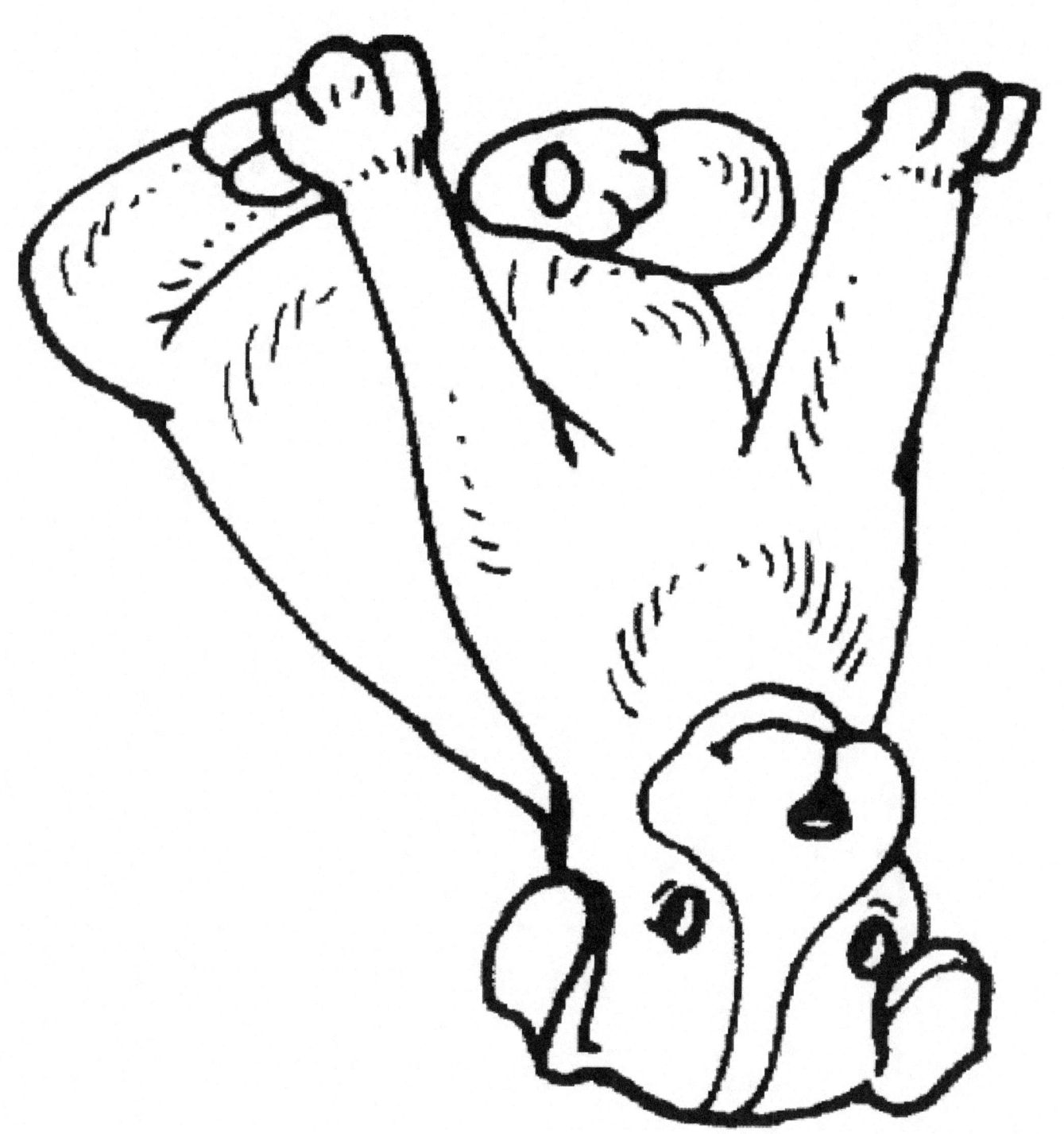